Chandrasekhar Kambar

Siri Sampige

NEW INDIAN PLAYWRIGHTS

Badal Sircar — *Three Plays : Procession Bhoma, Stale News*

Badal Sircar — *Beyond the Land of Hattamala and Scandal in Fairyland*

Vijay Tendulkar — *Ghashiram Kotwal*

Mahasweta Devi — *Five Plays*

Utpal Dutt — *The Great Rebellion*

Mahesh Elkunchwar — *Two Plays*

Mahesh Elkunchwar — *Party*

Mahesh Elkunchwar — *Old Stone Mansion*

Mahesh Elkunchwar — *Autobiography*

Satish Alekar — *The Dread Departure*

Chandrasekhar Kambar — *Jokumaraswami*

Chandrasekhar Kambar — *Samba Shiva —A Farce*

K. N. Panikkar — *The Right to Rule and The Domain of the Sun*

K. N. Panikkar — *Karimkutty and The Lone Tusker*

G.P. Deshpande — *A Man In Dark Times*

PERFORMANCE TEXTS

Rustom Bharucha — *The Theatre of Kanhailal : Pebet & Memoirs of Africa*

Also available:

Anuradha Kapur — *Actors. Pilgrims, Kings and Gods: The Ramlila at Ramnagar*

Richard Shechner — *Performative Circumstances from the Avant Garde to Ramlila*

David Hays — *Light on the Subject*

SIRI SAMPIGE

A Play in Sixteen Scenes

Chandrasekhar Kambar

Translated from the Kannada by
ROWENA HILL
with K. P. VASUDEVAN and N. S. RAMASWAMY

CALCUTTA 1992

Cover illustration by
Chittrovanu Mazumdar

Photographs courtesy Chandrasekhar Kambar

ISBN 81 7046 089 1

*Published by Naveen Kishore, Seagull Books
26 Circus Avenue, Calcutta 700 017*

*Printed in India by S. Das Gupta at
Sun Lithographing Company
18, Hem Chandra Naskar Road, Calcutta 700 010*

Contents

Introduction

Tradition is a much misunderstood word in India today. That it is a Western import (from the Latin *tradere* - to 'hand over' or 'deliver') is the last thing in the minds of those who believe themselves to be its votaries. What the urban Indian artist, desperately seeking his roots, is doing is not so much 'inheriting' tradition as 'inventing' it. Certainly this is worlds removed from native notions of *parampara* but let us clarify. In traditional art forms like music and dance we are still in unbroken contact with the past. But in modern art forms like 'drama' (to use an older nomenclature), it is a truism that what we have is really the anglicized Parsi theatre of the close of the century. It is the tradition of this theatre that has inspired the popular or commercial stage with its various gimmicks like the revolving stage, cyclorama and, of late, even shameless borrowings from the cinema much admired in plays produced in Madras.

It is against this background of groping for roots that Chandrasekhar Kambar's ethnic theatre has to be placed and evaluated. I still retain vivid memories of the explosive impact of his *Jokumaraswami* in 1972 in the alfresco setting of the back of Ravindra Kalakshetra that B. V. Karanth had devised for it. Something still needs to be said of the *bayalata* form in which this early play was so imaginatively clothed. *Bayalata*, as Kambar is never tired of repeating, is *total theatre*. It includes 'dance, drama, narrative, song, sex, death and religion' (Kambar, 'Folk Theatre As I See It'). Both the audience and the actors participate in 'what is ultimately a shared religious experience in the form of a play' (ibid). A traditional *bayalata* performance begins with prayer and ends with the audience as well as the players going to a temple early in the morning. Certainly *Jokumaraswami* began with a prayer; but it ended with a call for the birth of a more just society. Of course, Kambar is aware that in times of change *bayalata*—relevant only to organic, undivided societies—cannot survive. His subsequent experiments in theatre have taken him beyond *bayalata*. He has now turned to *yakshagana* and its possibilities for theatre today.

The revival of the *yakshagana* form owes a great deal to Shivram Karanth although many feel that he has 'bourgeosified' the folk form and trimmed it to suit Western and Festival of India audiences. By etiolating the form and removing dialogue altogether he has brought it closer to Western ballet and has, to quote theatre historian Rustom Bharucha, 'diluted rather than strengthened the energies of the "folk".' Marathi playwright Mahesh Elkunchwar has acidly characterized the borrowings of this theatre 'artistic kleptomania'. Kambar has tampered far less with the native form and his chief innovation has been the introduction of the playwright with its modern connotations. This has entailed a shift from the third person narrative of traditional *yakshagana* to a more dramatic form where the individual voices of the characters are allowed to be heard. The only restriction on the playwright is that he has to imaginatively enter into the world of the community's myths and deploy these myths to structure his plays.

Siri Sampige, the fruit of such a creative intervention into traditional practices (which is basically 'symbiotic' rather than 'parasitical' or so Kambar claims), was made possible through a Ford Foundation fellowship. The writing of the play began in May 1986, (the well-known *yakshagana bhagawathar,* Sri Prabhakar Hegde was summoned to Bangalore to assist in the process) and by July 1986 the first draft was ready. The scene now shifts to Heggodu, a tiny village in Shimoga, where the play went into production under the direction of K. V. Subbanna, 'the modest visionary', who has been the guiding spirit of the cultural organization Ninasam. The play was extensively revised and rewritten several times and suggestions from B. V. Karanth (who was present) were incorporated. On 20 August 1986 the play was finally staged in Heggodu and on 28 August the same year it was produced in New Delhi in the Ford Foundation workshop at Sri Ram Centre for Arts and Culture.

The question remains: How much does Kambar's *Siri Sampige* go beyond a traditional *yakshagana* performance to justify his claim that it is a legitimate extension of a basically religious form (with its attendant notions of *punya* for those witnessing it) into the secular domain of the 'modern stage'? In other words, have we here moved from the *celebratory* mode of traditional *yakshagana* to the *critical* mode of modern playwriting? Does the absence of a shared myth between audience and playwright automatically and unfailingly activate the critical consciousness?

A brief glance at the plot of *Siri Sampige* might be in order here. The

Prince of Sivapura, son of king Nagara Nayaka, has reached the age of sixteen when, on his mother's wish, he is to be married. But the Prince himself has fallen in love with the impossibly perfect lamp-maiden who comes to life one night in his bed chamber and disappears dancing into his own body. His account of this experience is couched in the most extraordinary terms and worth noting. He says that while he was 'all alone and fast asleep . . . the wall of this palace cracked, and someone drew a sword from its scabbard and let my thighs feel its edge'. He now demands that his body be split in two and the equal parts stuffed into two pots. Out of one he emerges unscathed (as he, according to prophecy, can only die if his brother dies and he happens to be the sole heir to the throne). But out of the other pot emerges, not the lamp-maiden of his dreams, but a hooded cobra. Marriage to Siri Sampige, daughter of king Pushparaja of Sevantipura, ensues but the Prince, in the grip of his earlier infatuation, will have nothing to do with his young wife. He periodically takes to visiting the lamp-maiden in a pool outside the town into which he gazes. Meanwhile Siri Sampige herself has been charmed by the snake-god, Kalinga, yields to him and conceives. Suspecting his wife's infidelity, the Prince orders a trial in which Siri Sampige proves her chastity. She takes the snake, which coils round the *nagalinga*, on her own body. She remains unharmed. In the end in a fit of jealousy, the Prince kills the snake and dies himself, fulfilling the ancient prophecy that he will die upon the death of his brother.

The play, then, recapitulates the growth of human consciousness from simple narcissism to full adulthood and genital sexuality. The symbolism of the snake is unmistakable,not only from the abundant Freudian literature but also explicitly in the play itself, when Siri Sampige becomes pregnant by Kalinga who turns out to be the 'rejected body' of the Prince. In the parallel sub-plot, involving the court jesters, Awali and Jawali, the sexual theme reappears: Jawali can make love to Kamala only when he turns into a snake. The negative influence of the Prince's mother on his sexual development (which we may broadly characterize his 'Oedipal' problems) cannot be ignored. Widowed when the Prince was barely a year old, the Queen Mother dotes on him and cripples him emotionally. The collective deaths of the Prince and Kalinga, as well as their thematic doubles, Awali and Jawali, may be viewed as the tragedy of the self-regarding narcissistic self. The play punctuates in wholly

Indian, non-derivative terms the passage to maturity. In achieving these larger truths through the use of indigenous myths, *Siri Sampige* goes way beyond traditional *yakshagana*..

T. G. VAIDYANATHAN

A Note on *Yakshagana*

This play is written in the form of *Yakshagana*. Narration is the soul of this form and it makes extensive use of song, mime and dance to create a total theatrical experience. The Bhagavata (narrator) tells the story in third person and other characters dramatize in the first person what he narrates. In the beginning, the characters have no independent existence; they are just a passive part of the narrative. Later they become full- blooded characters. While the Bhagavata is singing the story the characters interpret it through mime and dance. Later, they transform the same song into a dramatic event.

CHANDRASEKHAR KAMBAR

Siri Sampige was first produced in Kannada by Ninasam at Sivaramakaranth Rangamandira in Heggodu on 21 August 1986 and then at New Delhi at the Sri Ram Centre for Art and Culture on 28 August 1986 with the following cast:

PRINCE 1	Gopal Heranjal
PRINCE 2	T. Narayana Bhatt
KALINGA	Madhav Nayak
AWALI	Chandrasekhar
JAWALI	Manjappa
MOTHER	Sushila
SIRI SAMPIGE	Sudha
LAMP-MAIDEN	Sarada
KAMALA	Phaniyamma
BHAGAVATA	Prabhakar Hegde
ELDERS	Yesu Prakash
	Iqbal Ahmad
	Ganapati
	Prabhakar
	Srinivas

DIRECTION	K. V. Subbanna and Atul Tiwari
DANCE	Madhav Nayak and Gopal Heranjal
COSTUME AND STAGE	C. R. Jambe

The Hindi version of this play was produced by Goa Kala Akademi Theatre Art Faculty on 9 May 1990 and directed by B. Jayasree.

Scene 1

Bhagavata and the chorus.

BHAGAVATA *(Dedication)*

Before we speak, a thousand salutations
to you, great Lord Siva of Savalagi,
split in your divine play into man and wife,
dancing Nataraja Ardhanarishwara,
body and mind, spirit and matter you are,
split into two and beyond duality, hail Siva!
On Earth shining Sivapura's
King Nagara Raya is dead.
Queen Mayavati lives and rightfully rules.

Mayavati enters.

MOTHER Hear me! I am Mayavati, rightful wife of King Nagara Nayaka of Sivapura, city whose virtue shines upon the earth. My revered husband, after a long and virtuous reign, was borne away by time into timelessness. Since then I, like my revered husband, have continued to look after the interests of my subjects without the slightest flaw in my attention to them. And now to tell you of my household affairs, in brief. When my revered husband departed this life, our son Sivanaga was only one year old. As well as looking after my subjects, I took constant care in fondling and feeding him. I was happy watching his infantantics. From his fifth year onwards, my son received from the mouth of a teacher knowledge of all weapons and scriptures. Growing day by day like the waxing moon, he has now reached the age of sixteen, heir not only to his father's kingdom and treasury but also to his courage, daring and other virtues. Strong as a mountain, he is well fitted to be Lord of forest and field in this Kingdom. While I looking forward to being relieved of my worries after his coronation, one day a strange incident occurred. Hear!

BHAGAVATA Our family god spoke through an oracle, and
foretold his future. See! Two dangers threaten:
When his voice breaks he may become a monk,

When his brother dies, he also dies.

MOTHER How should it be that on a full moon day the milk to be offered to our family god was curdled, an inauspicious sign? While I was thinking with my head in my hands, 'Oh Siva, why should this happen?' our family god spoke through an oracle in the palace to tell me why. What he said was this: 'Daughter, there are two hindrances in the way of your son's good fortune. When his voice breaks, he may become a monk, and if not he may die because of one who is heir to what he is heir to'. On hearing his words, I anxiously grasped the feet of the god and said, 'Lord God, I will offer you the taste of palm wine, I will perform the five-torch ritual for you, I will build you a temple at Siva's right hand and place offerings at your holy feet. Let my son's family be a family of milk and gold; let him be without troubles, oh Lord!' Our family god blessed me with a small smile and said, 'When your son's voice breaks, arrange without delay for his marriage. Make sure he does not see his own image in water. Beware!' Thus saying, he vanished. Since I have borne no other child, my son's life is not in danger. But if the Prince sees his own image in water or in a mirror, he may become disinterested in worldly pleasure and riches and his mind may turn towards the ascetic life. Thus I myself have looked after my son with care so that he should not see his own image in water. My son is of robust beauty and lively. He can neither stand still nor sit still, but like a fresh young bull is always active, and I have seen the young girls of the clan sighing as they watch him. Just a few days ago his voice broke, and now we cannot delay any longer. After his marriage has been celebrated, he is to be crowned. To this the people have given their consent, but the Prince himself evades it each time with a new excuse. So many maidens have been shown to him, but still disappointed. I am worried now whether there exists anywhere on earth a maiden he can admire. The more he makes excuses and postpones the wedding, the more my worries and anxieties increase. The Prince has now to be called and forced into marriage. So be it. Listen, Bhagavata!

BHAGAVATA Speak, Lady!

MOTHER Send for the Prince immediately!

Enter the Prince

PRINCE Mother, I bow to your lotus feet. You sent word telling me to come immediately. For what reason, Mother?

MOTHER Son—

BHAGAVATA The Mother said, 'My Son, your voice
has broken so this is the right
time to marry. Hear me now —
wed a woman and rule the world,
please your mother and live long!'

MOTHER Child, you have to be informed of a very important matter; that is why you have been called. I am only a woman and becoming old, and I can no longer bear the responsibility of the kingdom, so I desire to celebrate your marriage in a way acceptable to you, witness your coronation and spend the rest of my life in peace. The Elders of the family have therefore been sent to Sevantipura to see King Pushparaja's daughter Siri Sampige, and have approved her as a bride for you. Now you must accept.

PRINCE Why do you want me to marry straightaway, tying a grinding stone round the neck of a child at play? Why should responsibility fall on me while there are elders living? Please don't make me unhappy, Mother, by constantly telling me such cruel things.

MOTHER Do not foster our anxieties, dear Son, by continuing to say no. Our lineage has been hurt with curses and sighs. You were raised with care and cunning, in order not to offend the pride of the family god or allow the eyes of the evil gods to fall on you. If some whirlwind sweeps away the plant raised by our sweat, then what will be the future of the lineage, my dear? Enough of the obstinacy you have shown lately! You don't want your mother's worries about your marriage to burn her to death with their pain, do you?

PRINCE Kindly do not speak such words, Mother! If you feel pain in your mind, please forgive me. Only because the maidens you chose all had some defect or other, I have refused to marry. For no other reason.

MOTHER Which maiden is flawless? Son, if you want such a maiden, then you yourself must be your own wife.

PRINCE I have faith that a flawless one must exist, Mother. From the day my voice broke, I have felt that she is hiding somewhere, like butter in milk. She is also trying to come out of her hiding place somewhere. Give me time to show her to you.

MOTHER Do you need time to tell me the name of the maiden you admire? Or is this just another excuse to postpone the marriage? That's enough. You shall have one week's time to say who the maiden is. If you give me her name, well and good. If not, you will marry Siri Sampige. Is that understood?

PRINCE Yes, Mother.

Scene 2

Enter Awali and Jawali, dancing.

BHAGAVATA You and I are a great pair of twins,
we two together play and sing,
Awali Jawali, Jawali Awali.
We smile, they all smile;
we cry, they all cry.
Those who never laugh will laugh with us,
those who never cry will cry with us,
the laughing pair, the laughing-stocks.

AWALI What sort of a Bhagavata is this? Doesn't he talk to the people who come in?

BHAGAVATA How should you be addressed?

JAWALI Hail, brave warrior!

BHAGAVATA All right, that's what we'll call you. What place are you from?

PRINCE To whom does Sivapura belong, have you heard?

BHAGAVATA To the King's mother, Mayavati Devi, so we have heard. Are you she?

JAWALI No, no! we are …

AWALI Those who make the cosmic egg and all lives that come out of such eggs laugh, or make them cry; the emperors of humour, the laughing-stock monarchs, the great twins Awali and Jawali. Do you know who we are?

BHAGAVATA No notion.

AWALI That's who we are.

BHAGAVATA Oh, so you are the twins! Between you two who is the elder brother and who is the younger one?

JAWALI I am the elder brother and he is the younger one.

AWALI No sir, I am the elder brother and he is the younger one.

BHAGAVATA Is there no agreement between you?

BOTH I am the elder or the younger brother.

BHAGAVATA This is like a riddle.

AWALI Sir, I will ask you a riddle, will you solve it?

BHAGAVATA What is it?

AWALI If this is there, that is not there; if that is there, this is not there. What is this, say?

BHAGAVATA I don't get it.

JAWALI So you give up?

BHAGAVATA I give up.

AWALI When there is a bride, there is no groom, and when there is a groom, there is no bride.

BHAGAVATA What does that mean?

AWALI You know the prince, our friend there are brides for him, yet if he is asked to marry, he refuses. And we men we want to marry but there are no brides for us.

BHAGAVATA There is a girl, will you marry her?

BOTH Oh, yes.

BHAGAVATA There's only one girl, how can both of you marry her?

AWALI Oh, you are right. Elder one, Jawali, you get married.

JAWALI Well, say I got married. Since you resemble me so much, my wife may go to bed with you mistaking you for me. What then? No, no, you marry.

AWALI What did you say?

JAWALI The same, as you just said.

AWALI I said you must marry.

JAWALI And I said you must.

AWALI *(with anger)* If I had a couple of fangs, I would have sucked your blood. I have spared you because I don't have them.

JAWALI *(with anger)* If I had a couple of horns, I would have run them through your belly. I have spared you because I don't have them.

Meanwhile a woman enters dancing. Both forget about fighting and stand staring, looking dazed.

BHAGAVATA Who are you lady?

WOMAN Oh, Sir, am I not the one who asked you to look for a bridegroom?

BHAGAVATA Oh, of course. Now, I remember but I've forgotten your name. What is your name?

WOMAN Should I say it again? Well listen: Mire is her birth place. Water is the place of relations. Looking at the man of light, she blooms. Say, what is it?

JAWALI Shall I say, sir?

BHAGAVATA Go ahead, my boy.

JAWALI Mire is your birth place,
Water of rains, your in-law's place
Man of light is your lamp.
Blooming one, aren't you?
Your name is Big frog,
Isn't it? Your name is Big frog.

All except Jawali laugh.

AWALI Look, how enthusiastically he exhibits his foolishness. Sorry sir. Shall I say it?

BHAGAVATA Yes.

AWALI She, who is born in the mire,
She, who floats on water
She, who blooms in light
Green moss, aren't you?
Hey, hey woman! Isn't Green Moss your name?

All except Awali laugh.

BHAGAVATA Can't you guess this much? Her name is Kamala, the lotus.

AWALI I knew it sir, but she looks lovely when she laughs, so I said that to make her laugh. *(Kneeling in front of Kamala)* Lady, to this much I swear, I will take the vow of obedient husbandhood for ever, and will serve you according to your dictates. This is the aim of my life. Won't you fulfil this wish?

JAWALI — My sacrifice cannot be less than this. Awali, I will sacrifice my very determination for your sake. I will marry her myself, right? Lady, won't you fulfil my wish? *(He too kneels in front of Kamala)*

AWALI — Why do you repeat all that I say?

JAWALI — That's exactly what I am asking you.

AWALI — You know how angry I am?

JAWALI — How angry?

AWALI — Very, that is, extraordinarily, that is, anger simply boils within me.

JAWALI — Boils? I will boil my grains in it. Please let me do it.

AWALI — How?

JAWALI — Say what I say. Now let us see. *(Slapping his chest)* Kamala is mine.

AWALI *(slapping his chest)* Kamala is mine.

JAWALI *(pointing Awali's fingers towards himself)* Say, she is mine.

AWALI *(pointing Jawali's fingers towards himself)* Say, she is mine.

JAWALI — Will you stop this and bark out something else?

AWALI — Will you kindly bark out something else?

JAWALI — I knew sir, that he was neither my elder my nor younger brother, that he was a rat or a bandicoot. Look how soon he has snapped the cords of brotherhood between the two of us.

AWALI — I knew sir, that he is neither my elder brother nor younger one and that he is a wolf or a fox. Look how he devoured the bond between us. I had decided to see the greatest fraternal disloyalty on earth and then die. I have seen it. I must die now. See you later.

BHAGAVATA — How will you come back to see me after dying?

JAWALI — He will somehow come back to kill me, sir. Hark, if there be any petty deities around, come and save me.

BHAGAVATA — Look, what is this? Do you think Kamala is a lottery? Isn't she the one to decide which of you she wants? Kamala,choose your man.

KAMALA — How is it possible, sir? Both are alike. Let them fight a duel. The winner is my choice, agreed?

AWALI — Agreed. Look, I am ready for the fight. *(To Jawali)* Hey, you huge stray dog, pig. . .

JAWALI — Don't reel out your titles in front of me. Come fight, quick.

Now take this.

Slaps Awali. Awali begins to cry.

AWALI Ah, ah . . . Oh my family god, save me. If you come here now, grant me this boon, that . . .

JAWALI Let Kamala be my wife.

KAMALA Amen *(She clasps Jawali's hand.)*

BHAGAVATA So, it is done. Kamala herself solved the problem. Now, I guess you both can live in peace.

AWALI How can there be peace now, sir? I will go to the forest, do penance and return a God to bestow the boon of death on both of them. Look, I am going to the forest.

JAWALI Wait, wait. First see us getting married and go there burning with jealousy. Sir Bhagavata, please bless us.

Jawali and Kamala bow to the Bhagavata. He blesses them.

AWALI *(in sorrow)* Hey sir, one last word.

BHAGAVATA What is it, son?

AWALI We have both served the prince, our friend, till now. Now, I am going to the forest. Ask him if he will carry on the work whole-heartedly. I say all this because when I imagine the prince without me, helpless and crying out 'Oh friend, Awali', . . . I feel overwhelmed with sorrow.

JAWALI Tell him sir, that if he leaves the city immediately, I will serve the prince with total dedication.

AWALI It is the prince's bedtime. Ask him to go and guard the prince.

Awali goes out weeping.

JAWALI Go, elder or younger brother, the river is dry. Fill it up with your tears. Let us see if it will begin to flow.

Scene 3

Bhagavata and the chorus.

BHAGAVATA Thus the Prince in Indranivas Palace
having lain down full of worries
—how can I believe my eyes? —
saw the carved lampstand come to life,

saying 'Beloved', beckoning,
inviting intimacy? Was that the wonder?
From the scabbard came the sword,
came alive between the thighs.

While the above song is being sung a statue of a woman bearing a lamp comes to life and starts dancing. The Prince is awakened, and while he attempts to catch the woman she vanishes, dancing, inside him. The Prince is in a state of high rapture.

PRINCE Oh! What a marvel! Could it be some goddess under a curse, turned to stone all this time, who has now rid herself of the curse and come to life again? Or some nymph who fell in love with me and hid in the stone waiting for me, and has now come out of her stone hiding place and blossomed into life? That creature who kept the burning lamp in her palm and leapt like flashing lightning has dissolved into my body! Is she suggesting that this is how I should get married? Yes, she must be the woman that satisfies all desires, who I have been longing for these many days. If that is so, I have found my bride. Friend, get up! I have found her!

Jawali *(waking)* You don't even let me sleep, man!

PRINCE Wake up quickly!

JAWALI How can I wake up any more than this?

PRINCE I've found the one.

JAWALI Who have you found? I'm right here.

PRINCE Uff! You don't understandme!

JAWALI Then tell me, man, so I can understand, who is the one you have found? Where is she? Have you hidden her under the bed?

PRINCE Stop joking. Please listen.

JAWALI Please speak.

PRINCE While I was fast asleep, it seemed that the wall of this palace cracked, and someone drew a sword from its scabbard and let my thighs feel its edge. I immediately woke and sat up, and dreams that were hidden in the corners seemed to spring up before my eyes. Wasn't there a figure of a woman bearing a lamp in that corner? Well, it suddenly filled with life, and its face bloomed with youth, and blossomed with a mysterious smile. While I went on watching it—no, her—she started to dance around me holding the holy flame in her palm. As she danced the sight of her flooded my limbs with pleasure and the pleasure became a creeper winding tightly all round my body and blocking my breath so that I was stumbling and in this tight embrace she dissolved into me.

JAWALI It sounds to me from what you say that it must have been the mischief of some female ghost. Dear friend, it would be good for you to keep a metal pot full of water beside your pillow. Do you know what for? So ghosts won't linger near you.

PRINCE This was no ghost, fellow. How can I tell you? Look, in that corner there used to be a figure of a maiden with a lamp, do you remember?

JAWALI Ah! where has it gone?

PRINCE Didn't I tell you? It came to life and dissolved into me while dancing. I am still perspiring with wonder. Run straightaway to my mother. Tell her to arrange a meeting of the Elders in the morning.

JAWALI At least let the morning come, man.

PRINCE No. Can't you see that it is dawn? Mother is worried. Go immediately, and tell her that the Prince has agreed to marry, with some conditions.

JAWALI What? You've finally agreed to marry? Who's the beauty?

PRINCE I'll tell you. First go and tell my mother.

Jawali exit.

Scene 4

In the Palace: the Queen Mother, Prince and Elders.

BHAGAVATA Elated as she heard the news, the Mother woke, circling hailed the family god; soon all were gathered together in the court, the Son arrived like the moon after an eclipse.

MOTHER Body and mind, mangled by horrid dreams, felt all the pleasure of the seven worlds at the news that our son had agreed to marry. On the wave of this pleasure, the Elders of the clan were brought forth to the palace. Thus our royal summons was sent, and none refused to hear it. All have come and are honoured in their respective places. Honoured Elders, our son has agreed to marry. He says he has some conditions. Being a woman, how can we handle this matter? You are equal in our eyes to gods. You, friends, must take care of this matter.

1st Elder — We are all happy at this pleasing news, Lady. Speak, oh Prince, make your desires known to all.

Prince — My Elders, to me, are not distinct from gods. Your desire is that I should be married, is it not? I agree to do as you desire. For the rest, you should agree to what I desire.

2nd Elder — We also agree.

Prince — It is I who will say which girl is to be my queen.

1st Elder — We are agreed.

Prince — In whatever form she is, you will get her for me.

2nd Elder — Wherever the maiden you desire may be, in whatever form she is, it is our responsibility to get her for you.

Prince — Do you swear by the family god you will get her?

3rd Elder — Yes, yes. We swear by the feet of the family god we will get her.

Prince — You have sworn. Your words are not different from the prophecies of gods. Do not ignore my words, thinking me only a boy, but listen carefully.

Bhagavata — Split, split my body into equal halves,
chop, chop it into even pieces.
Place at once those pieces in two pots!
Mother, comfort-giving Mother,
after a fortnight with your own eyes —
open, know and all rejoice.

Prince — Listen, I'll tell you. With this sword which you see before you, and with the family god as witness, I am to be split into two equal pieces.

Mother — Siva, Siva! Do not utter such inauspicious words, my son!

Prince — That is not all. After I have been cut into two, each piece should be stuffed into a pot. Both pots should be buried among flowers. On the next full-moon day, when you open the two pots, you will see come out of one a Prince of matchless charm, that is, myself. From the other will come the palace lamp-maiden, a woman of statue-like beauty holding a light in her hand. Then you should get the two of us married. If this is agreed, there will be a marriage. If not, no.

2ND ELDER We have seen many wonders and assimilated them. But of such an unlikely happening we have never heard.

PRINCE You have sworn before the family god, don't forget.

MOTHER This is madness, my Son. Some spirit has entered you to make you act like this.

PRINCE What entered me was not a spirit, Mother, but a beautiful woman in the form of a lamp-bearer. And this is the means by which she who has dissolved into me can be brought out.

MOTHER Can a human being who has been split in half come to life again? Can a woman be brought out of a dead body?

PRINCE It is possible, Mother. If you have the courage, and if you believe me, I will show you and you will see with your own eyes.

MOTHER Can we play childishly with such things? The Elders of the clan are not common men. Each of them knows a thousand wise sayings. You must act according to their experience.

PRINCE If the Elders act according to the word they have given, they are the equals of god and the fates. If they do not, they are the equals of human worms. If mother consents to this, she is the equal of the goddess of creation; if not she is the equal of the black goddess. If you agree to what I say, there will be a marriage. If not, you will see me leave here as a wandering monk.

The Prince rushes off.

BHAGAVATA Is the curse coming true, is our family's sin overflowing? Is our acquired merit wasted, has this lineage begun to burn?

MOTHER Oh Siva, I never expected that the punishment of fate would so soon leap upon me! Listening to my son's words, my fears were aroused to haunt me. Oh Elders, you know the history of our lineage from beginning to end. It is your responsibility to protect it.

1ST ELDER We have heard from legends and histories how in the past one or two kings of this lineage split themselves in two in this way. But now this situation has come about in truth and in our own lifetime! Console yourself, Lady! Now you are the one who must take heart and hearten others. We the Elders, not knowing the mind of the Prince, promised in the presence of god to do as he says. Or perhaps fate itself, unknown to us, made us utter those words. Anyhow, since the Prince has no brother to share his inheritance, there is no fear of his death. Whether your son is to become a monk will be a test of the strength of the family god, will it not Lady?

MOTHER Oh Elders, I have placed the scion of this family in your hands. Do whatever you will.

Scene 5

Mother and Elders.

BHAGAVATA In flowing light the Elders gathered,
the feet of all the gods were worshipped,
the Prince's body split and buried then opened.
See, what is this like the sun burning,
a precious gem its hood adorning,
lifting its hood like a big basket as it moves?
Saying 'Careful!' tittering, scattering,
Saying 'Hit it!' 'Kill it!' they attacked it.
Alas! They saw it disappearing into the forest.
Anxiously, the pot remaining
they raised and opened, calling on Siva.
The smiling Prince, the best of men came out.

PRINCE Where is the Lamp-maiden?

MOTHER What is this madness, Son? Listening to the words of your youthful rashness, we have done many things that we ought not to have done. All this comes from the curse on our lineage. Why else should it happen? By the blessings of the family god, you have come through to a new birth, at least. That is enough.

PRINCE Why? Did the Lamp-maiden not come out of the other pot?

1ST ELDER What came out was a hideous, horrible demon!

2ND ELDER An evil creature.

1ST ELDER A ghost.

PRINCE Cheated!

MOTHER Who is cheated? We are. For having tested thus the family god we will have to pay a thousand penalties. And now we all must make new marriage arrangements.

Scene 6

Kamala and Jawali in their house

KAMALA Husband, ever since our marriage, you have looked worried. Why?

JAWALI Marriage? Whose marriage? Mine? The King's? Or Awali's?

KAMALA Our marriage, that is, yours and mine.

JAWALI Oh, is that so? My love, last night in my dream, I was comparing you to a bird. But the comparison did not seem right because Awali had, on the same night, in his dream composed a poem in which he compared you to a bird. Please don't think of him too much, because then he appears in your dream.

KAMALA Husband, about your younger brother . . . why do you . . .

JAWALI Not younger, elder.

KAMALA What is Awali to you?

JAWALI Elder or younger brother.

KAMALA Well, your elder or younger brother is not here. Why do you hate him so much?

JAWALI Do I hate him? Impossible! To tell you the truth you are the apple of one eye and he of the other. I hold you both equal, you know? Because my elder or younger brother is not beside me, I am so afraid that I don't know what to say.

KAMALA Look into my eyes. *(He does so)* Don't you know what to say now?

JAWALI I do. But today in one of your eyes I see myself and in the other my brother has appeared.

KAMALA *(closing one eye)* Now look, who do you see?

JAWALI Awali.

KAMALA *(opening the eye she had closed and closing the other)* Now?

JAWALI Still Awali, even now.

KAMALA What is he doing?

JAWALI He is looking at you and sighing.

KAMALA Awali has become a ghost to worry you.

JAWALI Not a ghost, a wolf, a hungry wolf.

KAMALA Then imagine that I am a tiger, and the wolf runs away.

JAWALI Oh, no, no, you be Kamala. I'm more afraid of the tiger.

KAMALA You keep talking about Awali, why did you let him go?

JAWALI I wanted to finish him off. But what to do, the wretch is so much like me, you see, I thought, 'let me respect myself, at least' and let him go.

KAMALA O sir, this has gone too far.

BHAGAVATA What?

KAMALA You got us married. But instead of making love, all he does is remember his elder or younger brother and pine away for him.

BHAGAVATA Hey Jawali, I got you married thinking that you were a gentleman. If you go on doing this, I will have to change my opinion of you.

JAWALI What shall I do, sir? As soon as I look at Kamala with desire, my younger or elder brother appears in both her eyes. If I think of making love with the light off and our eyes closed, I get scared that he, who has hidden in her eyes, may rise up. That is why my eyes sting when I think of love.

BHAGAVATA But you can't ruin Kamala's life! Today is a Monday. Both of you go and consult your family god.

JAWALI Not today, the Queen has given me some urgent work to do.

BHAGAVATA What work?

JAWALI You must have heard the rumour about how my friend the prince sneaks out of the palace at odd hours?

BHAGAVATA We have.

JAWALI The Queen has asked me to trail the prince when he sneaks out and find out everything. After I come back, on some other day, we will go and consult the family god. Till then, I pray, keep your good opinion of me.

BHAGAVATA Well . . .

Jawali and Kamala exit, on opposite sides of the stage.

Scene 7

The Queen Mother and Elders in the palace.

BHAGAVATA Siri Sampige he married
but she could not satisfy him,
everywhere he went searching only for the Lamp-maiden.
The Prince's ever growing madness
made his ageing Mother worry,
'What god, what angel can protect our family?
Who'll guard our lineage in the future?
Lovely Queen Sampige Devi's
lotus face? how can I bear to look at?'

MOTHER So much we possessed, Elders, and what has become of it? I had hoped to spend the last days of my life gazing on my son as King and head of a family, playing with my grandchildren. How can Siva punish me so? They say that after marriage a son leaves the mother that bore him and falls under the spell of his bedfellow. No such thing happened here. I have not seen husband and wife laughing together even once. From the first day of their marriage, he would disappear at any time. Come back at any time. He goes off as if searching for something he has lost and returns as if hopeless at not finding what he seeks. He does not talk to anyone. When the family god was consulted, he sobbed and did not open his mouth to say anything. I cannot bear to see the face of my daughter-in-law, who is weeping all the time. My son's face I do not see. Tell me, Elders, what is to be done now?

1ST ELDER Does the prince eat from time to time, Lady?

MOTHER He eats, he does not eat. When he looks at me he turns his face away like a guilty person. Is it the family god's anger or the curse or possession by some ghost? I understand nothing.

2ND ELDER Where does he go, do you know, Lady?

MOTHER I don't know, but he returns filthy, as if he had been rolling in mud.

3RD ELDER Did you consult the astrologers, Lady?

MOTHER They say he is haunted by a female spirit. It may be true, because the day before he was split in two he said that the

Lamp-maiden of Indranivas Palace had come to life and danced before dissolving into him. What is surprising is that the statue has also vanished since that day.

1ST ELDER Has the prince looked at least once at his goddess-like Queen, Lady? If he had seen her, this problem would surely not exist.

MOTHER The problem, Elders, is deeper than you have realized.

BHAGAVATA Once not being able to see the Lamp-maiden in Siri Sampige's eyes
he said you are not the bride I desire —Go away!

MOTHER Once, and only once it seems, he started to stare at Siri Sampige's face. When she became shy and covered her face with her hands, apparently he rushed to her and pulled her hands away and caught her face in his palms, fixing his eyes on hers. But at once he said dejectedly, letting go of her face, 'There is no Lamp-maiden in your eyes, Lady', and left her. It is fortunate that the Lamp-maiden was not to be seen in her eyes. If he had seen her there, he might have plucked the girl's eyes out. Jawali has been sent to follow him without his noticing, to find out where he goes and what he does. Look, he is coming now.

Jawali enters and falls at the feet of the Queen Mother.

MOTHER Come, son. You must have found out the secret which is still hidden even after many servants have been sent to see. Tell me, where is the prince now? What is he doing? I am eager to hear, in detail. Were you able to follow him to the end?

JAWALI I was able to follow him, Mother, but what I saw there was terrible.

MOTHER That is what I want to know. Tell me!

BHAGAVATA Weeping, seeking the Lamp-maiden,
wandering over hill and mountain
to a pond he came then, thirsty for water.
Oh water, water, say who is she!
Is she not Lamp-maiden?
Saying 'I have her', he fell to the tempting reflection.

JAWALI Last night I followed the prince, according to your orders. It seemed the prince was going on a journey without preparations and without saying farewell to anyone. He went in fear, looking behind him, not seeing the way, stumbling, hiding wherever hiding places were to be found. Anyone who had seen him then would have said he was some criminal or convict fleeing, running away. Becoming thirsty, he went to a pond near the forest. The moon was out, and the sky was shining in the pond. Clouds had come up there, and beyond them infinite depths could be seen. He didn't notice that I had stolen up behind him and was standing there, and he looked into the pond. At the touch of his breath, as if angered, the water in the pond trembled and waves rose and broke up the reflected clouds and the deep blue sky seemed to be sliced by cruel knives. But my friend and Prince did not draw back. Until the play of the water was finished he remained still, and then again he looked at himself in the water. His reflection came up there like a floating corpse. The moment he saw it his face shone. Tears of happiness came to his eyes. In his ecstasy no word came from his mouth. As if silently talking with that corpse, he sat there, still.

MOTHER Strange! And then?

JAWALI He caught the reflection in his cupped hands and looked at it. The water spilled out between his fingers. Again he caught it and again it spilled. Then, as if the whole forest were crying, he raised his voice saying 'Maiden, Maiden!' and weeping.

MOTHER Did he say 'Maiden'?

JAWALI Yes.

MOTHER Did he weep?

JAWALI Yes, Mother.

MOTHER Listening to your tale has made me afraid, son. What should not have happened, what I was guarding against for sixteen years, has happened now out of my sight. The only difference is that he, who should have become a monk on seeing his reflection, is now thinking of the Lamp-maiden.

1ST ELDER This is a strange madness, one never seen or heard of before. There is no doubt about it.

2ND ELDER Have people lived who have loved their reflection in the water like this?

MOTHER My daughter-in-law is a thousand times prettier than that reflection, is she not?

3RD ELDER Reason cannot give an answer to madness, Lady. The Prince, in the bloom of youth, succumbed rapidly to the fascination of woman. The right thing to do will be to wait and see, Lady.

SERVANT The prince is coming, Madam.

MOTHER Let him come. Jawali, you two are boyhood friends. You can open your minds to each other. Try to find out the reason for his madness.

JAWALI Very well, Mother.

All exit except Jawali. The Prince enters. On seeing Jawali he is disturbed.

PRINCE What is it? why are you looking at me like that?

JAWALI It's nothing.

PRINCE I've gone mad — that's what you think, isn't it? But I can tell you that this is definitely not madness. My difficulty is that I cannot prove that all of you are cheats.

JAWALI Cheats? How have we cheated you?

PRINCE You said there was no Lamp-maiden anywhere.

JAWALI Yes. She wasn't found.

PRINCE So you say I was lying.

JAWALI Not lying . . . but she's nowhere to be seen.

PRINCE Yet she exists. Do you know I go out every day and see her?

JAWALI Do you really? Tell me all about it.

PRINCE You won't tease me?

JAWALI Do you doubt even your friend?

BHAGAVATA She came floating on the water,
beauty in the waves swimming —
could I cast a fishing line and pull her in?
Slowly slowly in the play of
ripples I saw the goal I was seeking.

PRINCE In that case, listen. Today I was beside a pond. She was inside it. She was swimming in the waves and ripples, glittering like a fish, moving her tiny arms. 'I must cast a line to catch her', I thought. 'No', I thought, 'I can catch her in my hand', and I stretched out my cupped hands. When my breath touched the water in my hands — do you know? — she trembled for love? Slowly she dripped down again between my fingers. Saying 'Silly girl!' I pinched her cheek. She laughed — do you know? — like lines running in the waves. Seeing her I laughed too, and I spoke. She also spoke as I did. Everything I did she did too, or everything she did I did too, there was so much harmony between the two of us that like two halves coming together we had become one. Gradually we became, both together, an indivisible zero, transcending form, becoming the Sivalinga, becoming God. Nor did the shadow of imperfect sorrow linger around this new god. Both of us together became this new god — ah! — it was like air, it was like light, it was like the blue of the sky, it was like empty space — it seemed it was impossible for anything physical to touch him. After seeing that god, I realized what beauty is and what ugliness is. Suddenly I felt that there is something lacking in this world we live in. Ah, God! It is a puzzle how we go on living with so much lacking in this world.

JAWALI Friend, is that god just sprouting a moustache?

PRINCE Yes.

JAWALI And is there a dark mole on his right cheek?

PRINCE Yes. How did you know?

JAWALI How could I not know? What you saw was your own reflection.

PRINCE Ay! Blast my foolishness in arguing with an ignorant person like you. Seeing one's reflection and becoming one with it means seeing the shape of the soul. But you can't understand all this. You are stuck to the body. People who refuse to see any further than the body cannot understand such things.

JAWALI To me 'body' means an empty stomach, and 'soul' means a full stomach. What do you say?

PRINCE What? Are you teasing me?

The Prince looks for some time at Jawali, annoyed at his apparent teasing, then goes off dejectedly. Jawali follows him.

Above The young prince (Gopal Heranjal) recounts his dream vision of the beautiful lamp-maiden and *(below)* relives the experience of union with her (Sarada).

The prince is split into two.

Above The prince after the split (T.Narayana Bhatt), in a contemplative mood. *Below* The twins Awali (Chandrasekhar) and Jawali (Manjappa) provide comic relief.

The queen mother (Sushila) expresses her sorrow at the travails besetting her family.

Kalinga (Madhav Nayak) makes his entrance from the netherworld.

Kalinga approaches and woos Siri Sampige (Sudha).

Kalinga finds himself unable to duel with his brother, the prince.

Above The prince is reconciled with Siri Sampige before he dies at the feet of his distraught mother *(below)*.

Scene 8

Enter Kalinga

BHAGAVATA Ask not where he went — the Serpent
has made its dwelling deep inside you,
go not searching for your lost one
living deep inside the anthill of the mind *(to Kalinga)*
Bravo, sustainer of the serpent lineage!

KALINGA Who does the nether world belong to, do you know?

BHAGAVATA We have heard it is Lord Kalinga.

KALINGA We are that Lord.

BHAGAVATA For what reason do we suddenly see you here?

KALINGA Aahaaah! We the traveller and acclaimed great hero of the eight directions and the fourteen worlds were resting once after our daily duties in our palace in the nether world, when a girl's voice appeared to be calling us. While we were wondering how a woman's voice could be making itself heard in a bachelor's palace, as if descending to plunder our world she appeared before us. Losing all sense of ourselves, we knelt before her. Was it a dream or was it real? Such a thing might perhaps occur once in a while, but that was not the case here; every day we saw the same vision. Why should we be thinking about a woman who belongs to someone else? But that also did not seem to be the case. She seemed to be our rightful wife, known to us for a long time. From the day we saw her, the desire to possess her stirred in us. Very well. We decided to go in search of her.

Sampige appears.

BHAGAVATA Oho! Is this the lovely beauty,
she who appeared to us in visions?
If she won't be mine my life is wasted;
till my dying breath I cannot give her up.

KALINGA Aahaah! So where was she, the girl who seduced my mind? I went round searching every region of the earth, but she is to be found here in the backyard of Indranivas Palace in Sivapura. There she is, the girl over there. She's the one who stole my mind away! Even at this distance the smell of ploughed earth that her body exhales makes me tingle. Aha! She is not an easy woman. She must be the prettiest in the province! All right. I will go up to her and make myself visible.

BHAGAVATA Who is this comes riding up
my body, who is he that I
don't know, but yet upon my mind
is printed?
Wherever I go I see arise
and stand by me his handsome shape
and longings of desire are born
to trouble me.

SAMPIGE Who is he? As if the five elements came together and took shape, he came walking from the direction of the anthill. For quite some time he has been chasing me; wherever I go he is looking at me with hungry eyes. Wherever he steps, sparks seem to fly. I do not know him, but he appears to be already etched on mind, and as I see his handsome form my desire rises. Longings I had not known before are now standing with their mouths open. Who is he?

BHAGAVATA Pleased as if he's found a treasure
Kalinga swollen proud and vain
says whether she is maid or wife
she must be mine, I'll plunder all
her joys.

KALINGA Aha! Her body is like a festival for my aroused senses. It seems to be beckoning. Big buttocks, big big breasts! Small waist, pool of pleasure! Eyes trained in hunting. Whether she's maid or wife, even if my life is lost in the attempt, it doesn't matter. Unless I bed her, my life has been wasted.

BHAGAVATA One must not yield to base desires —
it's fitting to advise him so.
He ran up, she stopped him, but she looked,
and fell under the wizard's spell.

SAMPIGE I have become like a boat caught in a storm and overturned. Someone is opening the doors of my youthful breast, and shaking all my desires to awaken them. No, I must not sacrifice my judgement to such base desires. I will talk with that man who is coming to seduce a woman belonging to another, scold him and send him away.

She goes a little further forward and hides. Kalinga also goes running toward her. Sampige closes the door and stands at the door.

SAMPIGE Who are you that chooses a time when no one is near and comes to chase me wherever I go? It is the Queen of this country herself who you are provoking! You must be a shameless rogue to dare as much!

KALINGA Aha, your voice is like honey, my lovely. Your angry words sound sweet. You make me want to catch and kiss the words as they are born from your mouth.

SAMPIGE Answer the question I asked you. If you try any mischief I'll tell the King, and he'll have you chained and dragged through the streets.

KALINGA You have already bound up my heart and mind with your long hair, girl. The only thing left is for you to put chains on my body with your smooth arms. And I am prepared for that.

SAMPIGE The intoxication of youth has gone to your head. It seems you don't understand civilized words. Wait. Mother! *(She shouts.)*

KALINGA You are a good actress. When I came you shut the door, and now you are pretending to call someone to protect you. Your kind of woman finds force very attractive, I know. So here you are!

MOTHER *(from outside)* Siri Sampige!

SAMPIGE The Queen Mother has come. If you want to live, hide!

KALINGA Don't talk so proudly. I can protect myself. If you have any courage, open the door!

SAMPIGE My virtue is in my own hands. Who should I fear? Look, I am opening the door. Guard yourself.

Sampige opens the door. The Queen Mother enters. Kalinga immediately changes shape, becoming the King.

MOTHER What a surprise. Husband and wife together and happy! Day and night I do penance to bring that about! Son, on my eyes dried up from joylessness, you have showered the rain of a new joy. Wait, wait! I will straightaway make a sacrifice of an eight-legged animal to the family god. Son, Siri Sampige is very delicate. Do not make her shout again with your roughness, do you hear?

KALINGA *(resting his arm on Sampige's shoulders; she moves away from him)* We'll tame her. Don't worry, Mother. Sampige only called you for fun, didn't you my Goddess?

SAMPIGE Yes. No, no, I really called. *(Aside)* So much joy wells up in me at his touch. Who is this wizard who has come to plunder me?

MOTHER Son, stop your roughness. Siri Sampige is already trembling like a flowering creeper.

KALINGA What is an eight-legged animal, Mother?

MOTHER It means a pregnant animal. I will sacrifice so that our Siri Sampige will quickly give me a grandson. In the pools of her eyes I can already see suffused and shining the golden colour of tomorrow's dream. If you stand here like this, my evil eye may fall on my dear daughter -in-law. Close the door.

Exit Mother.

SAMPIGE Before madness overcomes me, please tell me who you are. You were like a hissing snake, and now you are like the Prince. How many existences do you have?

KALINGA As many as you want. Look into my eyes, girl. Am I like your Prince?

SAMPIGE True. The Prince is a little effeminate to look at.

KALINGA A little! Quite a lot.

SAMPIGE It was to search for the woman inside him that he split himself, wasn't it?

KALINGA In that case, now tell me—am I a stranger? While you were in bed with your husband, who was lying there like a piece of wood, was there not in the nether regions of your mind a king kneeling before you, begging for your love?

SAMPIGE Yes.

KALINGA That was me. Did you recognize me as King Kalinga, ruler of the nether world in the depths of the Prince's palace?

SAMPIGE Yes. No, no. I don't know who you are.

KALINGA But I know you. I can even tell you what dreams you dream. And I will teach you the dreams that you shall have from today on. Come on now, dreams, let us see. There is a forest, and in the forest there are flowers, tender leaves, trees full of fruit . . .

SAMPIGE Yes, there is a forest, there are fruit trees . . .

KALINGA In fresh sunlight a golden river is flowing.

SAMPIGE A river is flowing.

KALINGA You have come to fetch water.

SAMPIGE Yes, I have come to fetch water. Here in the ground there is an entrance like a burrow.

KALINGA Descend.

SAMPIGE Aah! How fine this world is. How many coffers of gold there are in the nether regions. In every corner so many nameless joys are sleeping freely. Ay! a sevenhooded snake is standing like a lamp-stand aiming its raised hoods at me. What can I do?

KALINGA *(taking his true form)*: Don't be afraid, girl. I am yours.

Scene 9

Jawali and Bhagavata

JAWALI Hey, Bhagavata!

BHAGAVATA What?

JAWALI Shut one eye and look at me.

BHAGAVATA I looked.

JAWALI How many people am I?

BHAGAVATA Only one.

JAWALI All right, now open both eyes and look at me. How many people am I, tell me.

BHAGAVATA Only one.

JAWALI What, Bhagavata, sir! You are making fun of me. If with one eye we see one man, with both eyes we should see two men.

BHAGAVATA Is that so? In that case how many people do I look like to your eyes?

JAWALI Two.

BHAGAVATA How?

JAWALI You and I. You and your shadow. Awali and I. That's why

I sometimes feel as if I had four legs. Don't you, Bhagavata?

BHAGAVATA You are lucky and I am unlucky. I have only two legs.

JAWALI You are also lucky, Bhagavata, sir. Do you want to know why? In front of you let us assume that there are two paths. By keeping one leg on each you can walk down both paths.

BHAGAVATA Bravo, bravo! We did not know that at all. So you walk down four paths at the same time, do you?

JAWALI I? No, Bhagavata, sir, but I have seen with my own eyes, Bhagavata, one man walking at the same time down two paths.

BHAGAVATA Is that so? Who is that fortunate person?

JAWALI Our Prince. He is to be found with the Queen in the women's apartments, and at the same time he is to be found near the pond as before, looking at the god reflected in the water.

BHAGAVATA How can that be?

JAWALI Think of my position! At times he recognizes me, and at other times he turns his face away like a stranger. If I see him in the women's apartments, he becomes confused and asks me 'who are you?' If I go to the pond, he calls me 'friend' and embraces me. If I tell him, 'You didn't recognize me in the palace, friend,' he says 'I didn't go to the palace at all!' Let's say that one hand may not know what the other hand is doing, but isn't it strange that one leg doesn't know the path that the other is walking?

BHAGAVATA It is strange.

JAWALI When I told him, 'The Queen is going to have a child, you will soon be the father of a prince, you should give your poor friend a tasty dinner of game', his eyes widened and he looked at me as if he would tear me apart and devour me!

BHAGAVATA What joyful news you bring! The Queen has become pregnant! Couldn't he at least have handed out sweets to me, the Bhagavata?

JAWALI Of course, I have brought them sir, take this. Keep distributing them to all who pass by. I will go and get the things for worship.

BHAGAVATA Why things for worship?

JAWALI Look, the very lotus of my heart has bloomed and is

approaching us. Ask her.

Jawali goes, Kamala comes. Awali who has entered from the back stands unseen.

BHAGAVATA What is this Kamala? Are you on your way to offer worship? What is the matter?

KAMALA Sir Bhagavata, though it is years since we married, my Lord, my husband does not love me. Without love how can there be its fruit, a son, the boon of progeny? I leaned on the pillars of my house, a month on each, sighing and crying out to God. Just the day before yesterday, we were blessed with the grace of the family God. He appeared in my dream and instructed me in this manner—'My daughter, on the anthill, under the banyan tree, outside the city, there is a creeper of blooming jasmines. If you first worship, then pluck the flowers, make a garland out of them and put it round your husband's neck, he will transform himself into a serpent and unite with you. If you unite in this manner you shall have children, not otherwise.' So we are going there now.

BHAGAVATA Well, may your wish be fulfilled.

As she leaves Awali steps in front of her.

AWALI Lady, I have a request.

KAMALA What, you are still standing here! Did you get the bael leaf?

AWALI But you never asked me to.

KAMALA Look, the old madness again. Now, will you get the leaf or not?

AWALI But there is no bael tree near by.

KAMALA Husband, isn't there a bael tree near the east-side window of our house?

AWALI Which is the east window of our house?

He goes off, searching. Jawali enters from the other side with the leaf in his hand.

KAMALA Now, where did it come from? Well, well, no need to explain, get the fruits and flowers.

JAWALI Oh, sure.

He goes out, Awali enters.

AWALI Look, the bael leaf.

KAMALA But you've brought that already, what I asked for were fruits and flowers.

AWALI Okay, I'll get them.

As he leaves Jawali enters from the opposite side. Seeing both of them standing face to face, Kamala becomes alarmed.

BOTH Hey, there is a mirror in front of me.

Both act as the object and the image.

AWALI Mirror, mirror have you an eye, too?
Or, has my eye become a mirror now?

JAWALI Is that you seeing me?
Or, is this I seeing you?

AWALI Am I your image? A shade?
Or are you my image? A shade?

JAWALI Without me you are not there, is this true?
Or, without you I am not there, is this true?

AWALI Apart we two may be,
Yet, down below the tree's root is one.

JAWALI Between us is glass.
when broken, the two ends and we are one.

AWALI If two ends, do you get one?
Or, is it lonely we get?

JAWALI Melting, in each other,
Can we live, in the mind doesn't the glass remain?

AWALI The words we have heard till now . . .

JAWALI You tell me! A dialogue or a soliloquy?

BOTH *(recognizing each other)* Aren't you my elder or younger brother?

AWALI How are you, my elder younger brother?

JAWALI Kamala, go in immediately. I will speak to him and come in.

BHAGAVATA Oh, isn't one of you two Awali? Are you here too, Awali? What were you doing all these days?

JAWALI He has done the worst possible things. *(To Awali)* Will you go away now or shall I have a go at all that fat in you?

AWALI I have as much of a right as you have to both this house and Kamala.

JAWALI *(to Bhagavata)* Tell him Bhagavata sir, that he is like a bear rushing into the shrine when worship in going on.

AWALI *(to Bhagavata)* Tell him Bhagavata sir, that he is the zenith of stupidity.

BHAGAVATA But look, I am confused myself. I don't know,which of you two is Awali and which Jawali? To whom shall I say anything? Lady, Kamala, you tell me, which is your husband?

KAMALA I am confused too. Suggest a means to find this out.

BHAGAVATA Well then, do this. Our elders used to say that the hearts of those in love beat faster. Hold your ear near both their hearts. The one whose heart beats faster is your husband.

Kamala does so.

KAMALA Both their hearts are beating like your drums, sir.

JAWALI All right, let another duel decide this. You, you fox, who come slinking in to chew up the sugarcane in my garden, I am ready to hunt you. Take this, face it.

AWALI *(stepping back in fear)* Why should a duel always decide?

JAWALI *(trimphant)* My love, do you know how replete with virtues of valour and fearlessness I am? Or should I give you a taste of it, too?

KAMALA I know now, my lord.

JAWALI Then come now for worship, towards the anthill.

Kamala and Jawali go out.

BHAGAVATA You went to perform penance, didn't you?

AWALI I went. I performed the penance, too. After seeing God, I came back.

BHAGAVATA Really? How is God? Doing well?

AWALI God means a huge, big fire-pit of arrogance. He is arrogant because the atoms of dust and blades of grass, even the sun and moon are under his control. Devotees keep pouring the ghee of devotion and the pit keeps glittering with fire. You know, sometimes there are contests between the emperors and God. I thought this very petty and came back here.

BHAGAVATA Lucky man. You had a great enlightenment.

AWALI Sir, I want a buffalo. Is there one in your chorus?

BHAGAVATA There are many in the city. Why do you want a buffalo?

AWALI I need a pot of milk.

BHAGAVATA Why milk?

AWALI — To give my brother food, make him eat a gummy plum and drink up that milk.

He exits.

Scene 10

BHAGAVATA — The god who showed smiling
in the water dripping from cupped hands
has gone back to the depths.
The prince is stunned.
When he came with empty hands,
the body that was revealed he did not recognize,
and asked 'who are you, rogue?'

Prince enters, desperate.

PRINCE — Whatever I touch becomes foolishness; whatever I look at becomes deception. It has reached the point where even the clown is laughing at me. *(Siri Sampige enters.)*

SAMPIGE — You look grief-stricken, my Lord.

PRINCE — Yes. Believing I was certain to see the god, I went out with a light burning in my eyes, but I have returned in darkness. I thought that God may give us pain enough to make us cry, but now all forces have joined in the mischief of darkness so as not to allow any light to come near me.

SAMPIGE — You may have refused my love, but look, my arms are still wide open to receive you, leaving the past behind.

PRINCE — How innocent your face is, my Lady. It is a freshly blossoming lotus without a speck of mire on it, your face. But look at my face. As I pictured the god in the water, the mire below was thrown up at it. The body is pure, my Lady, but the soul is dirty. Sins are visible to the soul.

SAMPIGE — You need rest, my Lord. If you sleep a little while, and have beautiful dreams . . .

PRINCE — So I should still close my eyes, is that what you suggest? Well, you have dreams, you are fortunate. In reality you are a Queen and in dreams you are a lover. You can handle the selves of two worlds. But I—the day I was deceived by the god, I lost my dreams too, Lady.

SAMPIGE — What does that mean, my Lord?

PRINCE — Rejecting my body, leaving it with you, I went to the pond to see the god. What came floating in the water was neither the Lamp-maiden nor a god. It was not even my reflection, Lady, it was my corpse. And that was what I held daily on my lap and ate of. The more I ate, the hungrier I felt. I ate more and more of it, and by the time I realized it was a corpse, it was too late. When I repented and came back, my body itself had vanished. In the meantime someone had entered it and gone off with it. Now I am almost air, Lady, I cannot even make your skin feel my touch; I don't exist except as air that speaks. I need a body to show myself in. My hunger for life is growing. Lady, I need a body. Please help me.

SAMPIGE I am a slave at your feet, my Lord.

PRINCE I don't want that. If you help me sincerely, that is enough. Can't you co-operate with me?

SAMPIGE Of course I will, my Lord.

PRINCE You must not break your word.

SAMPIGE No, my Lord.

PRINCE Are you sure?

SAMPIGE Yes.

PRINCE Will you swear on my life?

SAMPIGE I swear on your life.

PRINCE Then look! *(Shouting)* Hey! who is there?

SAMPIGE All are sleeping, my Lord who will come?

PRINCE It is the King of this country himself calling.

SAMPIGE It is midnight, my Lord.

PRINCE But a great truth has been revealed to the King of the country at this moment. Who is there?

SAMPIGE If anyone hears, what will they say? Stop it, my Lord.

PRINCE You are a partner in this truth. Be quiet. Who is there?

The Queen Mother and a servant enter.

SERVANT What are your orders, your Majesty?

PRINCE Come, Mother. Servant, go now without delay and beat the drums. I know it is midnight, but do not argue with me. Go and proclaim that tomorrow morning all the citizens and heads must assemble in the Nagalinga temple. The Queen Sampige Devi will undergo a trial.

Exit Servant.

SAMPIGE Trial? Why?

PRINCE To reveal the truth of your illicit pregnancy.

MOTHER Prince, you are not in possession of your senses. Before whom are you speaking thus?

PRINCE Before my Mother, who believes the Queen's lies, and before Queen Sampige Devi herself.

MOTHER Siri Sampige has told no lies.

PRINCE Please forgive my irreverence, Mother. That foetus in her womb is not mine. To whom does that poison belong? That is the truth that must come out.

MOTHER I say that it is yours.

PRINCE That is not true, Mother, It's deception.

MOTHER How sure can I be of the truth? If it is true that you are my son, then it is equally true that the child in that womb is yours.

PRINCE How many truths are you handling, Mother? I cannot manage even one truth. Since that foetus bears my name, I have the last word, Mother.

MOTHER You are half mad. You are not fit to bear witness.

PRINCE That is why I said it should be decided in public.

MOTHER Your madness is spreading beyond all limits. Now you are making a private affair into a public issue.

PRINCE Before the law all are equal, Mother.

MOTHER This is the height of insanity. *(Painfully)* My eyelids are heavy with the weight of life. Son, I can bear no more.

PRINCE I too have grown old, Mother. It seems I was always two, and the one that I have lost somewhere must be my elder brother or my enemy. You have kept hidden from me the secret of his existence, like this one, keeping her secret in her womb and wrapping her sari round it. Perhaps you did the same.

MOTHER Prince, no such great catastrophe has happened. Do not lose your judgement in unnecessary hatred.

PRINCE Even my hatred is split in two, Mother. I cannot wholly hate the Queen. And he who in my absence illicitly was joined with her, who brought a treasure without anyone knowing and hid it in her womb—I have no wholehearted hatred for him either, Mother. Admiration, and jealousy yes, but I need him. That is why tomorrow morning the

Queen's deception must be exposed. As King I have announced it. Tomorrow morning you too must graciously attend.

Prince rushes off.

Scene 11

In the temple of Nagalinga: Mother, Sampige, Prince and the Elders

BHAGAVATA Honouring the great men who attended
the King bowed and said thus:
'Breaking palace laws Sampige's womb
has quickened. Say, is it right?'

PRINCE To you, the great of the earth, my devout salutations and thanks for your attendance!

1ST ELDER We are flattered by your modesty, Lord!

PRINCE In my inexperience I am facing a dilemma regarding social duty. So I was obliged to call on you, the equals of gods, to guide me.

2ND ELDER Even the family god will be touched by the decisions that the King takes in the presence of the Elders. We will conscientiously say what is true and right. Please speak, Lord.

PRINCE What should be the punishment for a woman who has abandoned her husband, has illicitly joined with another, and has become pregnant? Let the final word be said.

1ST ELDER First of all it must be proved that the pregnancy is illicit, Lord.

PRINCE And what is the evidence to prove this?

2ND ELDER The inmost conscience of husband and wife is the evidence.

PRINCE And if there are people who can deceive even this inmost conscience?

1ST ELDER Then the final proof is a trial by ordeal, the form of which is to be decided before all.

PRINCE In that case, decide. The woman who has committed a crime here, and is illicitly pregnant, is the Queen of the country, and the one who is asking for justice is the King. *(All are shocked.)*

1ST ELDER Oh Prince, we have heard you are not in good health. If that is so, it is natural for your mind also to be disturbed. A problem of family prestige such as this can be solved before the Queen Mother, who is like the family god to us all. This is not a public problem. This is our feeling.

PRINCE When citizens require justice, the King provides justice. When justice for the King is needed, the Elders should provide justice. That is social duty.

2ND ELDER The King rules in two realms. One is the earth, the other is his wife. So the final authority with regard to justice or injustice in both is his.

PRINCE Since in the eyes of justice all are equal, and the King himself is in need of justice, I am requesting you to decide. If you still hesitate, it is against your Elder status.

2ND ELDER You should not force the disturbance of your body and mind upon the Elders, Lord. There is still time. You can consult with the Queen Mother and thus take a proper decision. This we humbly pray you to do.

PRINCE What is the proof that my body and mind are disturbed?

MOTHER The unspeakable words you are saying—is that not enough? The soot you are throwing on the history of our family — is that not enough? You are the owner of the body and the mind of the Queen. Not being able to answer for both—is that not enough?

PRINCE My words are the words of sorrow of one who has suffered an unjustice. Don't you understand?

1ST ELDER Your intervention with your advice, Lady, is what will serve best here. Once, some time ago, becoming witnesses to the splitting of the Prince, we allowed our eyes and minds to be wounded. We are not prepared now, in witnessing this madness, to be wounded in our souls. Look, we depart.

PRINCE You are forbidden in the name of the family god to take one step forward.

2ND ELDER For the misfortune of being Elders, must we also become partners in all your sins?

MOTHER Keeping in mind the truth of the gods, I pray before all the clan for fortune to favour us. Great efforts must be made to protect the truth, Elders. If we neglect it even for one moment, the truth will fly out of our hands, and this thousand-year-old lineage will collapse. To the man who gives up his judgement for his pride —forgetting his proper destiny and his duty—to this kind of man it is difficult to discern a woman's truth. If everybody's truth was to be at the level of their own noses, what would happen? Fortunately it is not so. Elders like you are here to give a discerning judgment. That is our good fortune. Knowing that this is an insult to a woman, still I insist. The blessings of the family god will prove my daughter-in-law's truth fullness. Please see the trial and give your judgment. Afterwards perhaps my son's madness will be cured.

1st Elder — We have no doubts in accepting the Queen Mother's judgement. Let the Prince accept also that there is to be no second opinion about our judgment.

Prince — I agree.

2nd Elder — In that case, listen. Our words are the words of gods. Let the Queen herself decide what the form of the trial should be. We have faith in the Queen's wisdom.

Bhagavata — The king cobra writhing in play
on the linga I will take on my body.
If I am pure it will go away,
otherwise it will sting me.
Do you agree?

Sampige — Look, that snake which is crawling there on the Nagalinga—I will let it climb on my body. If I am a pure and virtuous wife, it will move over my body without stinging me and go away. Otherwise it will use its poison and sting. By this trial the truth can be tested and punishment be given at the same time. Is it acceptable?

Elders — We accept.

Mother — Come, daughter.

Bhagavata — With hands joined above her head
she came before the snake linga
bowed and trod devoutly round the idol.
Abandoning fear she stretched out her arms;
saying 'Snake, protect the truth,
come to me', she took the snake upon her body.
Were they friends, she and the snake?

Did the dumb creature know the truth?
Showering the Queen with kisses, charming,
opening its hood it played on her,
the light in its hood-jewels gleaming,
happily twined with her plait, her womb caressing
turned its hood-light to the front
slipped down the slope of her thighs
and seeking its linga master moved away.
All the people stood like painted beings.
'A strange thing we saw', they said,
'truth depicted by the Queen's grace for us all.
Hail, oh hail, to our godlike Queen!
Hail to a mother's faithful womb!
Hail to the lineage!'
All bowed to Sampige.

The Prince rushes up to the Nagalinga, but the snake is no longer there. He searches for it, then stands amazed.

MOTHER By showing us this miracle, Siri Sampige has become an angel.

3RD ELDER What you have done, Lady, has spread the glory of earth up to the Heavens. Our country is blessed.

1ST ELDER A hundred salutations to the Queen. A thousand victories to the Queen's truth. Wherever the Queen's feet step, may towns and temples rise.

All join their hands in a salute and go up to the Mother, bowing. With the Mother, they go to salute Sampige. Then all exit. Only the Prince remains behind.

PRINCE This is cheating, cheating!

Scene 12

BHAGAVATA Without the elder the younger brother died.
'Life has no meaning any more;
from now on I cannot live', Awali said and wept.

AWALI *(crying)* Alas! My younger or elder brother is dead! Now I am all alo-o-one. I no longer have any near or dear ones. Oh God!

PRINCE Who is that weeping so terribly?

AWALI I, Awali.

PRINCE Why are you weeping all alone?

AWALI Because I am alone, that's why.

PRINCE Where did Jawali go?

AWALI He went and died on me.

PRINCE He died? When? What happened?

AWALI You know that anthill under the banyan tree outside the city? Well, he had gone there with Kamala to worship.

BHAGAVATA Inspired by greed, this man too went there with a pot of milk and lay in wait.

AWALI Not that, I went to bathe the Sivalinga with milk.

PRINCE And then?

AWALI After worship Kamala took the jasmine garland on the linga and put it round Jawali's neck. As soon as she garlanded him, Jawali turned into a serpent.

PRINCE Don't lie.

AWALI I'm not lying. Ask this Bhagavata if you want.

BHAGAVATA It is true that Jawali turned into a serpent. The family God had instructed thus.

AWALI As soon as he became a serpent, he began the love-play with Kamala. Later, he even proceeded to do things, which, out of shame, I can't mention. Gradually, with accelerated pleasure, they both began to pant like flood water rushing down into a valley. To cater to the fatigued and hungry ones, I made a small fire and put the milk on to boil. The milk got heated and started to boil. The boiled milk began to overflow. The smell of the overflowing milk reached the serpent inside Kamala. The serpent came out. Since he was hungry, he spread his hood and dipped his mouth right into the pot. His mouth was burnt and he died writhing badly.

BHAGAVATA Sheer lies my Lord. He killed Jawali.

AWALI Maybe. But I did so because I felt that he would kill Kamala, lying speechless there.

BHAGAVATA A lie again. Blinded by jealousy and anger, seizing the opportunity, you chopped the writhing snake whose mouth was burnt with an axe.

AWALI *(weeping)* Alas, I killed my elder or younger brother with my own hands.

PRINCE Don't cry. Tell me what happened after that. What did

Sampige do?

AWALI Not Sampige, Kamala. Through the horrors she lay still, her eyes closed in intoxicated pleasure. I filled the pots with the serpent bits and threw it out. I cleaned up the blood, woke up Kamala and told her sweetly, 'Come, let us go home'. She thought I was Jawali and began to walk with me. Slowly, she walked a few steps and then sat down saying she was tired. After a while she got up to walk. Gosh, what do I see! She had laid an egg where she had sat down. Angry, because it was the serpent progeny, I crushed it between my hands.

BHAGAVATA You did that out of your jealousy for Jawali.

AWALI The one who has seen it seems to know better then the one who has done it. Well, you describe everything, then.

PRINCE Tell, sir.

BHAGAVATA He crushed the second egg too in the same manner. But when he crushed even the third, Kamala came to know. As soon as she knew, the contentment and pleasure in her eyes disappeared and she began to tremble with anger enough to fill the seven worlds. The pearl - ornament on her nose split into bits. Milk streamed down from her breasts like tears and her blouse became wet. Screaming in a terrible voice and shouting, 'Wretch, you have destroyed my progeny' she tore her loosened hair, threw it at him and disappeared into the forest. Even the sun set.

AWALI *(weeping)* Oh, alas, I have become lonely now . . .

PRINCE Don't cry. You also wanted him to be killed, didn't you?

AWALI Yes.

PRINCE He's dead and gone. Isn't it better for you?

AWALI As long as he was here, I wanted to kill him. He was always here or there, behind or in front of me, near or far from me. But now without him I have become half myself. That's why I feel I too should die. I am alone.

PRINCE Hey, Prince!

AWALI Prince?

PRINCE Don't get frightened. I thought you were I. You are fortunate, at least you are alone. Look at me. Even when I am sitting alone, I feel there is someone like me sitting next to me, wandering around in my body, talking in my voice, stealing me. I thought it was not a man but a mirror, but he is not a mirror, because a mirror cannot talk, and he talks. A mirror will not move by itself, but he wanders all through the palace, not caring about me. I will tell you a secret, don't tell anybody. He has stolen my wife also, and slipped into her bed. Wait! Did you hear? His voice from the women's apartments of the palace?

AWALI: Yes, I hear the voice of some man in the women's apartments.

PRINCE: Don't make any noise. The Queen is bathing his face with the light of her eyes, washing away the stains of his sin, thinking that their last moments together should be pure. But I suffer day and night remembering their sins, and roam longing and thirsting for his blood.

AWALI: Shall I bring servants to catch the enemy?

PRINCE: Go! But bring them without making a sound.

Scene 13

The palace. Sampige nursing the child. Kalinga watching.

BHAGAVATA Siri Sampige's child I'll go and see,
talk to it and return, said the Snake King.
He crossed the fence and was there.

KALINGA Won't you speak, Sampige?

SAMPIGE Why have you come? The Prince suspects me. He doesn't go to the pond any more but guards me like a servant. Don't you understand?

KALINGA I had to speak to you.

SAMPIGE Well, you've spoken to me.

KALINGA I wanted to see the child's face.

SAMPIGE Look at the child's face. Now you can go.

KALINGA Just one moment. Give me a chance to talk to you once more, Sampige. Look what has happened to me. My eyes have had no sleep. I do not know where the boundaries of my kingdom are. I just sit around, forgetfully wondering 'Will she look at me once at least?' The walls of the fortress you have built to keep me out are growing taller.

SAMPIGE I also have my responsibilities and my honour, Kalinga. Please go away.

KALINGA Remember, my goddess. Remember the dark boy who played with your hair. Sometimes you would say, 'Kalinga, dear snake!' and sometimes you wanted me to become the Prince. Using both of us you set your womb alight. Wooing my mind with smooth talk you won your trial. Now, after using me, do you want to throw me away like a spent firebrand?

SAMPIGE My body is not a commodity, Kalinga. For you that child may be an extension of your pride in yourself, but for me it is a wound you have given me.

KALINGA It is difficult to understand you, woman.

SAMPIGE Now I am worried for your life, and I am telling you, escape from here at once.

KALINGA I have come here for the last time to tell you something, then I'll go. If I don't tell you, I may not even be able to die.

SAMPIGE Why do you talk like this?

KALINGA It is true, Sampige. Who else do I have but you?

SAMPIGE Are you afraid, Kalinga?

KALINGA Of whom, of the Prince? When I see him I don't feel angry at all. I don't know why. Maybe my own entrails continue in him. Maybe we were brothers in a previous birth.

SAMPIGE You wanted to tell me something. Tell me, I will listen.

BHAGAVATA A frightful shadow, dear,
is haunting me;
an eagle is stalking me,
biding his time.

KALINGA Listen, Sampige. I am surprised at how I have spent so many days with you. I started feeling that I was desiring some shadow beyond you, or that I had caused it some pain. Whenever I lay with you that shadow beyond came to tease me. All these days I forgot it only in the momentary happiness of the body. I mean to embrace you in such a way that not even air can slip between us, but between us there remains a huge empty space. And in that space the dark shadow appears, beckoning to me. Before, I saw your body. Now I see nothing but the shadow. That shadow is the truth between us, I feel.

PRINCE *(from outside)* Close everything. Lct a soldier with a weapon stand at each window and passageway. Remember, the enemy is a wizard who can take on any form he wants. Lady, open the door!

KALINGA Now my mind is lighter. I will go now, Lady. Open the door.

SAMPIGE I will open the door slowly, singing a lullaby. Escape by the gutter. No one is standing that side.

BHAGAVATA Cobra with his seven hoods,
in every hood a diamond gem,
snake entwined in a girl's plait,
in her plait adorned with jasmine,
sleeping cobra, hushabye,
hush, our cobra King, hushabye!*

Scene 14

Prince and Awali.

BHAGAVATA Open the door, you harlot!
Who are you playing around with?
I'll chop that rogue in pieces, roared the Prince.

AWALI When the door was opened there was nobody inside. Even when we searched according to your orders, in every nook and cranny, nobody was caught.

PRINCE Did even a worm escape?

AWALI Only a snake escaped by the gutter drain. We who were ready to hunt men thought that if we chased the snake the enemy might escape, so we didn't go after it.

PRINCE What was that snake like?

AWALI When it got down into the garden it threaded its way like a stream flowing. Then, as if concerned that someone might see it, it looked all round, moving its hood. And the hood was really very impressive.

PRINCE Were there not memories of joys devoured in its eye?

AWALI We could not see its eye, friend.

PRINCE When you saw it, did it not seem born in heaven?

AWALI Yes. It moved with the poise of a thousand kings.

---

* *An alternative and longer sversion of this song is included in the Appendix.*

PRINCE — Did it shine in the sunlight, like a comet walking on the earth?

AWALI — It shimmered like wheat, and its head was like lightning. Moving like the emperor of the forest, as if to show us the grandeur of the darkness, it disappeared inside a darkness-filled anthill.

PRINCE — Was this not the same snake which the Queen took on her body that day at the trial?

AWALI — How can I tell, friend? I am not properly informed about animals.

PRINCE — Fool! Just as you could detect Jawali's secret pleasures, I also can detect the enthusiasm of that snake wherever it moves. Its royal poise proves that it is the same snake as the one which was there on the day of the trial. And if it is definitely the snake of the trial, then it is also definitely my enemy. He can take on any form he wills, and now, scared, he has run away as a snake. Go! If he enters an anthill, set fire to the anthill; if he enters the forest, set fire to that too. Even if you have to mix poison with the air we breathe, he must be caught and killed.

AWALI — I am going. *(He exits.)*

BHAGAVATA — Aha, she came, Siri Sampige,
lover inside and Queen outside,
deceit in female form came out, came out.

SAMPIGE — What is this my Lord? You appear to be prepared for battle.

PRINCE — Lady, do not cover up the truth with smooth talk. Tell me did not a snake escape from here just now?

SAMPIGE — Yes.

PRINCE — Is it the same snake that moved around on your body on the day of the trial?

SAMPIGE — Yes.

PRINCE — Speak, then! Is not that snake your lover?

SAMPIGE — Yes.

PRINCE — In that case what you have been doing all this time is immoral.

SAMPIGE — At last you have come to know of it. I am glad. I was wondering all the time how I could reveal it to you.

PRINCE — You cheated the Elders, you cheated everyone. You

wounded them in their faith in you, didn't you? Your name which has been that of a goddess of town and temple will become a term of abuse for the whole country, do you know that?

SAMPIGE That is your ill fortune. My immorality started, my Lord, when you forgot the body and began craving for the god, and slipped away from our bed. I who was lying on the bed, counting the rafters in the roof and sighing, never noticed when you slipped away. I searched for you, but wherever I searched, in the palace garden, or in the words you spoke, you were not to be found. In the end you saw the god by taking handfuls of water from the pond. I too took a handful of water, and there was a god in my handful too, but if he turned out not to be the same god as yours is it my fault?

PRINCE Do you know the punishment for immorality?

SAMPIGE I am already half widow, my Lord. You can't understand the grief of one who is always half a widow! When you split yourself you split me also. When you are before me, my body is widowed; when I am with him, lying with him, my mind is widowed. Thus I am always half widow. There is nothing to equal such a torture. My sorrow is that no one understands me. I am alone. Afraid of loneliness, I search for a companion. But all the companions to be had are half men. Was I born for half men? I was born for and I am seeking the wholeness of the linga of the god Siva. But what fell to my lot was a child born illicitly to an incomplete being. A child born to a widow. You have come here to kill the woman who gave birth to an illegitimate child? Look, I am ready!

Enter Awali.

AWALI Friend, the trace of the enemy has been found. He is hiding in an anthill. The soldiers are already digging up the anthill.

PRINCE Lady, I have better work for my weapons. After beheading my enemy I will come and dispose of you. Do not hope that I will die in battle. Since I have no brother, I cannot die.

Exit Prince and Awali.

SAMPIGE Now I am a complete widow.

Scene 15

A battlefield. Prince and Kalinga face each other.

BHAGAVATA You who lay with my woman,
You who polluted my lineage,
till I kill you I will not cease, roared the Prince.

PRINCE Are you not the one who came like a wizard and lay as an adulterer with my woman? Are you not the dog who has polluted my lineage? Until I have killed such an adulterous thief as you, how can my weapons rest quietly? Come and give battle, lowest of the low!

BHAGAVATA In the mirrors of eyes I have seen you
You are like my other self;
anger at you will not rise in me,
brother perhaps in a previous birth.

KALINGA Keep away, Prince! I am not one who is afraid to fight. I remember seeing you many times in a mirror. Pity wells up in me whenever I see you. Give me time, Prince, before battle, so I can think why I feel so troubled.

BHAGAVATA Coiling up like a snake —
I don't understand this disguise —
I am your destiny's eagle,
resist, he said.

PRINCE You who cheat by taking on any form that suits you, you need more time? You are scared for your life, shrinking, and coiling up, but none of your plots will succeed any longer. Look, the eagle of your destiny is going to fall on you now. If you have courage, defend yourself!

KALINGA Prince, do not provoke my pride. You are delicate. You have only read about killing in poetry. Give me once, only once, a chance to look you in the eyes.

PRINCE To do that would be the same as to give you a rope to tie my hands with. So what now? Are you going to fight or are you going to die like a coward? Lookout, fight!

BHAGAVATA Enraging each other, fighting,

with roars their bravery flaunting
both fought mightily their awful battle.
At last, the Snake King's entrails aching
he opposed his foe less strongly;
the Prince like thunder felled him
stamping on his body.
Gazing at the sky's distance
life flew from the Snake spirit;
in his open eyes the Prince
saw a wonder unforgettable.
Looking there — ah ha — himself
he felt his spine's knot slipping;
'My entrails have gone cold' he said
coming to the palace.

Scene 16

The palace. The Queen Mother is waiting for the Prince.

BHAGAVATA News of victory can't make her happy, she remembers all her nightmares; with eyes wet Mother was waiting at home.

MOTHER Even after hearing the news of the Prince's victory, my mind is anxious. If I shut my eyes I see only bad dreams, and if I open them bad omens arouse the fears in the depths. The palace is reverberating in silence, like a thunderstruck tree. Look, the Prince has come. The Prince enters and offers his salutations to his Mother. My child, may you be victorious over a thousand such enemies.

PRINCE This is not such a great victory, Mother. *(He feels pain and sits down).*

MOTHER No, my son. I never thought the Queen could cheat like this.

PRINCE Where is Siri Sampige, Mother?

MOTHER She must be hiding in some corner, covering her shameless face. Do such people not commit suicide, son?

PRINCE I feel that at this moment the Queen should be with me.

MOTHER What kind of Queen is she now? She lost that position at the moment when she polluted the lineage. Should you look at her evil face at such a time of gladness like this, my child?

PRINCE There is something private I want to talk to her about.

MOTHER I, your mother, am with you. Is that not enough?

PRINCE You stay with me. Let her come too. Who is there?

SERVANT *(Enter)* Lord, what is your command?

PRINCE Ask the queen to come. And call Awali too. I must have a word with him.

SERVANT Awali died, my Lord.

PRINCE Awali died? When? How?

SERVANT When you were fighting, Awali came running to us shouting, 'Alas, I am tripping over her hair, free me, free me'. We, who were busy watching your war did not pay any attention. Moreover, his feet were not tangled with hair. He kept running and went towards the lake which you visit every day. Meanwhile, as expected, you killed the enemy. I too ran towards the lake to tell him this joyful news. Awali had already begun to climb the tree on the bank that bends over the water. The tree's reflection was in the water. Awali's reflection had appeared too. Suddenly, he remembered Jawali and the quarrel and he thought that the one in the water was Jawali. Seeing Jawali, he grinned at him menacingly. In the water, Jawali too laughed to show that he was not afraid. He too laughed, and raised his arm, threatening to strike. The other did the same. He clenched his teeth and indicated that he would strangle the other. The other did the same. He became extremely angry and determined to kill, he jumped right into the lake. I watched all this, standing on the bank. I thought that he was probably miming your fight. But he drowned after having drunk so much water. He did not come up at all, my Lord.

PRINCE *(agitated)* Go at once and ask the queen to come, quick.

SERVANT Very well, my Lord.

Exit Servant.

PRINCE How is my son the Prince, Mother?

MOTHER You are tired after the fight. Take some rest. It is already dark outside. Your mind will be lighter when you get up in the morning. If you want you can see Sampige tomorrow.

PRINCE Mother, are you saying that tomorrow will dawn?

MOTHER What kind of a question is that my child? Tomorrow will dawn, but not as usual. Right and wrong will be in their proper places. The darkness of doubt will have passed away. Do you know, there will not be a corner of the palace where the light does not fall. Dawn has only to awaken, and the buds of a new world will open out. All the old grief will blossom into smiles. I myself will show to you, king upon your throne, the new world.

PRINCE Mother.

MOTHER Son.

PRINCE Do you have faith in me, Mother?

MOTHER From now onwards I will believe every word you say, my child. Because I did not believe your words on the day of trial, all these terrible things came about. A Mother who does not believe her son's words is virtually a black goddess; but I will never forgive Siri Sampige for cheating like this.

PRINCE Now there are no secrets between us, may I ask you a question, Mother?

MOTHER Ask, my child.

PRINCE Listen calmly. My navel is growing cold. My spine is loosening.

MOTHER *(horrified)* What? What did you say, son? Who is there? Servants! Someone come quickly!

PRINCE Don't shout, Mother. Please listen to me.

MOTHER Watching your face I am becoming scared, my son. I am a sinner not to have realized at once. I thought it was the fatigue of the fight. Did he wound you?

PRINCE Listen, Mother. Even my death depends on the truth that you must tell me. You must reveal the hidden truth now.

MOTHER What is it? Ask me, my child.

PRINCE Is it true that I have no brother to be heir to what I am heir to, Mother?

MOTHER Do you doubt your Mother's word? Look, I swear on the family god . . .

PRINCE Oaths and vows are not required, Mother. You can simply tell me.

MOTHER You have no brother, my son.

PRINCE I am to die together with my brother, is that not so?

MOTHER Yes.

PRINCE Suppose I have no brother?

MOTHER Then you will not die.

BHAGAVATA Splitting ourselves we became two body and mind became separate.

PRINCE No other may have been born from your womb, but when the one son who was born from you split himself in two, did not the other part which came to life become my brother and the sharer of my inheritance? Tell me, Mother, the other who came to life when I split myself, who was he? When I asked all of you, you said it was a devil, an evil spirit. Was it not the Snake King Kalinga, Mother?

MOTHER *(stricken)*: Yes. What came out of the pot before you was a snake!

PRINCE Mother, think carefully. Was he not the same snake who was used for the trial?

MOTHER Perhaps . . .

PRINCE Certainly he was the same, Mother. He did not fight with me as he should have. He said, 'Somehow I cannot get angry with you. Give me a chance to look into your eyes'. But I refused his request and fought with him, and since his heart was not in the fight I easily killed him. He died opening his eyes and looking at the sky. I could not control my curiosity and looked into his eyes.

MOTHER What did you see, son?

PRINCE In his eyes the lovely blue sky was reflected. I saw in the sky an eagle and a snake flying together. The snake, which had within it all the dark black secrets of the nether world, was not in the claws of the eagle but was wound around its neck and body in friendship. The duality of the snake and the eagle had been erased and they had become one. The mercy of Siva's divine eyes was falling on them in the form of the sun's golden rays. What I saw now was like a snake playing in the sky, opening his hood. Only the snake was visible, having completely taken over the eagle, and it looked as if the snake with its open hood had sprouted wings and was flying. Then that eagle, with its forehead set to the streaming sun, climbed fearlessly into the eternity of the sky.

MOTHER Son, what do you mean by this?

PRINCE The Queen would have understood all these things. Siri Sampige has not committed any wrong, mother. When I split myself, we got separated into body and mind. Kalinga became my body, I became his mind. Siri Sampige became pregnant by my body.

MOTHER *(in wonder and repentance)* True, son. That is why whenever he wanted he was able to take on your shape. Son, the Queen has done no wrong. Alas! sinner that I am, I forgot what I was doing. Now I am afraid for your life. Who is there?

PRINCE I have already killed myself, Mother. Look, the Queen has come. Come Siri Sampige.

Sampige approaches.

MOTHER Is no one coming? Siri Sampige, you stay at the Prince's side. I will go and bring the doctor.

Exit Mother.

PRINCE You who were being burned in the fire of misunderstanding . . . at last I feel I have understood.

SAMPIGE Are you well, my Lord?

PRINCE Queen, how is the Prince?

SAMPIGE He is sleeping quietly. How are you, my Lord?

PRINCE Did you hear the news?

SAMPIGE Yes, my Lord. You killed Kalinga.

PRINCE Have our Prince perform the last rites for him. For me also.

SAMPIGE My Lord!

PRINCE Listen. See to it that our son does not split himself. *(He dies.)*

THE END

Appendix

Hushabye Our Cobra Lord

Kalinga is the name of a cobra
who has seven hoods,
seven gems like seven sun-cubs
sit in his seven hoods.

He waves his hoods and tail
whenever he sees a girl;
to see a little girl with oiled plaits
makes Kalinga very pleased.

He entwines his body in the plaits
and swings like a plait himself;
if the girl has jasmine in her hair
he nods off happily.
Hushabye, our Cobra Lord!

If he sees a shadow he flies into a rage
and hits it with his hood,
flings his gems at the fleeing shadow,
flicking his forked tongue.

Once our Kalinga in fresh sunshine
stretched out his length;
an eagle's shadow big as a mountain
touched his snake body.

He burned with anger, his eyes threw sparks,
he displayed his seven hoods,
and thrashed that shadow wherever it went
with his hoods, like a thunderbolt.

Thrashing, from his hoods the fresh blood flowed;
his hoods shrivelled and shrank,
his eyes became charcoal, his body a rag,
his tongue a loose thread—
hushabye, our Cobra Lord!

Bury him in flowers, bury him in dreams—
hushabye, our Cobra Lord!
Shoo shoo, eagle, fly far away,
my child is sleeping sound.
Hushabye, our Cobra Lord!